Letts

KS2 Success

Age 7-11

Maths

Test

Practice Papers

Trevor Dixon

Contents

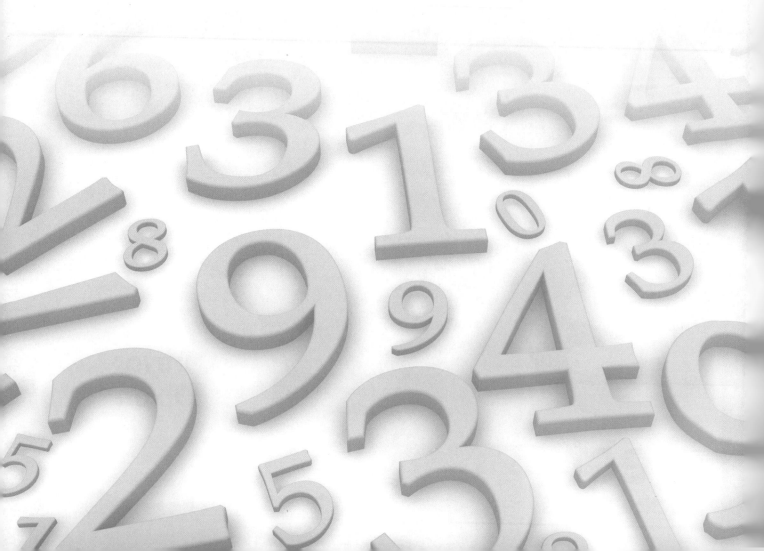

Introduction and instructions

How these tests will help your child

This book is made up of two complete sets of practice test papers. Each set contains similar test papers to those that your child will take at the end of Year 6 in maths. They can be used any time throughout the year to provide practice for the Key Stage 2 tests.

The results of both sets of papers will provide a good idea of the strengths and weaknesses of your child.

Administering the tests

- Provide your child with a quiet environment where they can complete each test undisturbed.
- Provide your child with a pen or pencil, ruler, eraser and protractor. A calculator is **not** allowed.
- The amount of time given for each test varies, so remind your child at the start of each one how long they have and give them access to a clock or watch.
- You should only read the instructions out to your child, not the actual questions.
- Although handwriting is not assessed, remind your child that their answers should be clear.
- Advise your child that if they are unable to do one of the questions they should go on to the next one and come back to it later, if they have time. If they finish before the end, they should go back and check their work.

Paper 1: arithmetic

- Answers are worth 1 or 2 marks, with a total number of 40 marks. Long multiplication and long division questions are worth 2 marks each. A mark may be awarded for showing the correct method.
- Your child will have **30 minutes** to answer the questions as quickly and carefully as they can.
- Encourage your child to look at the number of marks after each question to help them find out how much detail is required in their answer.
- Where questions are expressed as common fractions, the answers should be given as common fractions. All other answers should be given as whole or decimal numbers.

Paper 2 and Paper 3: reasoning

- Answers are worth 1 or 2 marks, with a total number of 35 marks. A mark may be awarded for showing the correct method in specific questions where there is a method box.
- Your child will have **40 minutes** to answer the questions as quickly and carefully as they can.
- Encourage your child to look at the number of marks after each question to help them find out how much detail is required in their answer.
- If your child needs to do some working out, advise them that they can use the space around the question.

Marking the practice test papers

The answers and mark scheme have been provided to enable you to check how your child has performed. Fill in the marks that your child achieved for each part of the tests.

Please note: these tests are **only a guide** to the level or mark your child can achieve and cannot guarantee the same level is achieved during the Key Stage 2 tests.

	Set A	Set B
Paper 1: arithmetic	/40	/40
Paper 2: reasoning	/35	/35
Paper 3: reasoning	/35	/35
Total	/110	/110

These scores roughly correspond with these levels: up to 49 = well below required level; 50–69 = below required level; 70–89 = meets required level; 90–110 = exceeds required level.

When an area of weakness has been identified, it is useful to go over it and to look at similar types of questions with your child. Sometimes your child will be familiar with the subject matter but might not understand what the question is asking. This will become apparent when talking to your child.

Shared marking and target setting

Engaging your child in the marking process will help them to develop a greater understanding of the tests and, more importantly, provide them with some ownership of their learning. They will be able to see more clearly how and why certain areas have been identified for them to target for improvement.

Top tips for your child

Don't make silly mistakes. Make sure you emphasize to your child the importance of reading the question. Easy marks can be picked up by just doing as the question asks.

Make answers clearly legible. If your child has made a mistake, encourage them to put a cross through it and write the correct answer clearly next to it. Try to encourage your child to use an eraser as little as possible.

Don't panic! These practice test papers, and indeed the end of Key Stage 2 tests, are meant to provide a guide to the level a child has attained. They are not the be-all and end-all, as children are assessed regularly throughout the school year. Explain to your child that there is no need to worry if they cannot do a question – tell them to go on to the next question and come back to the problematic question later if they have time.

Maths

Paper 1: arithmetic

You **may not** use a calculator to answer any questions in this test paper.

Time:

You have **30 minutes** to complete this test paper.

Maximum mark	Actual mark
40	

First name	
Last name	

Date of birth	Day		Month		Year	

1   43 × 5 =

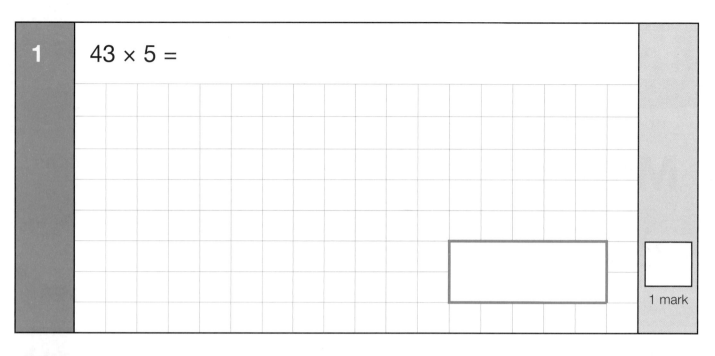

1 mark

2   574 + 56 =

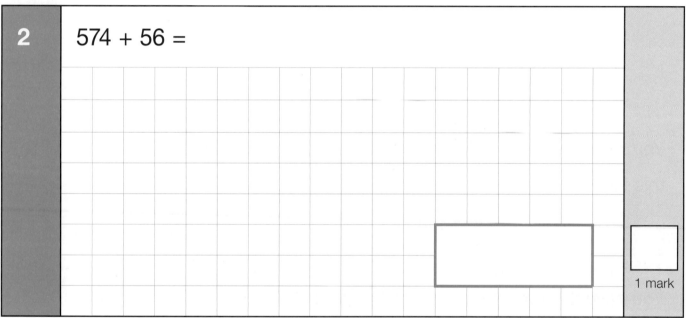

1 mark

3   1,234 + 100 =

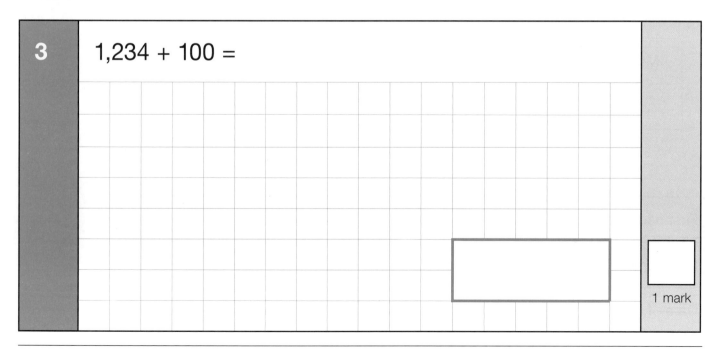

1 mark

4

$$\frac{2}{5} + \frac{2}{5} =$$

1 mark

5

9,999 – 1,000 =

1 mark

6

5,868 – 2,434 =

1 mark

7

607 × 3 =

1 mark

8

8.1 ÷ 10 =

1 mark

9

45,054 + 32,876 =

1 mark

10 $5^2 =$

1 mark

11 $9{,}345 \div 3 =$

1 mark

12 $\dfrac{9}{10} - \dfrac{1}{5} =$

1 mark

13

$10 - 15 =$

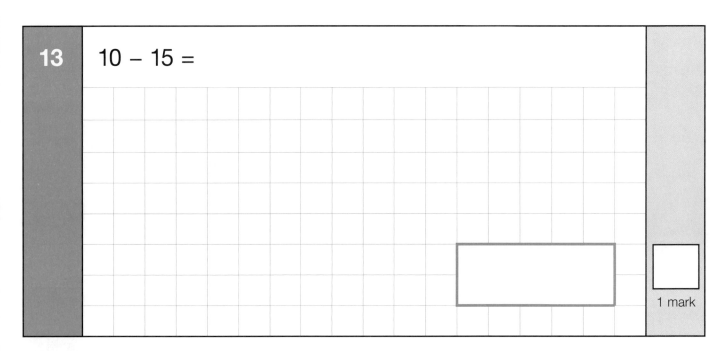

1 mark

14

$\dfrac{1}{2} + \dfrac{2}{5} =$

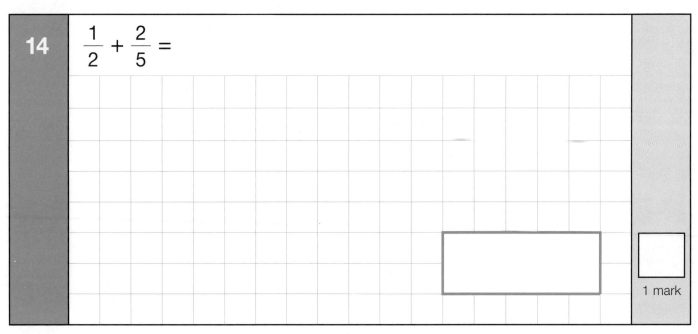

1 mark

15

$\dfrac{1}{3} \times \dfrac{1}{2} =$

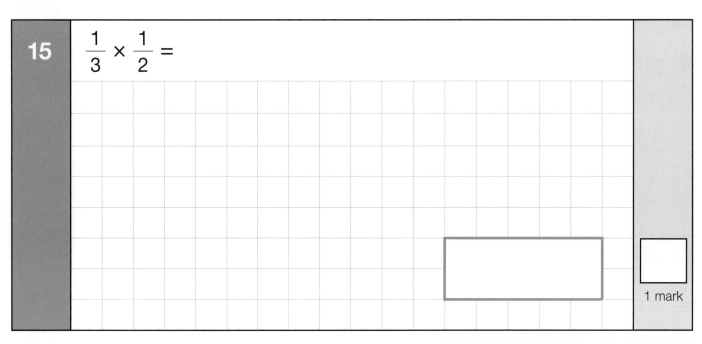

1 mark

16

$$\frac{1}{2} \div 4 =$$

1 mark

17

$$0.6 \times 4 =$$

1 mark

18

50% of 2,500 =

1 mark

19

$50 - 5 \times 10 =$

1 mark

20

$45,725 + 63,750 =$

1 mark

21

$825,804 - 235,075 =$

1 mark

12

22 47.32 + 215.44 =

23 486.48 − 39.57 =

24

Show your method

```
    2 3 4
×     2 6
```

2 marks

25

Show your method

```
2 3 ) 5 5 2
```

2 marks

26 $30.75 \times 100 =$

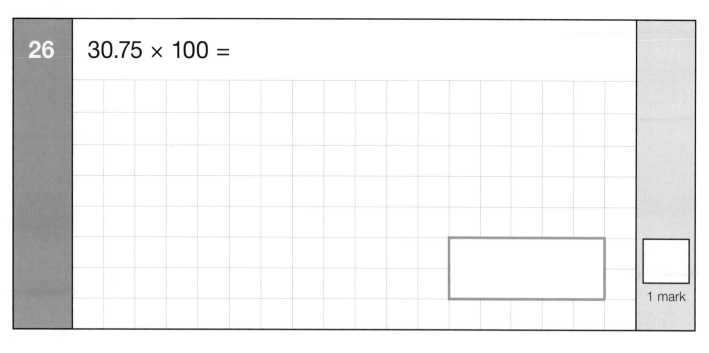

1 mark

27 $\dfrac{3}{4} + \dfrac{4}{12} =$

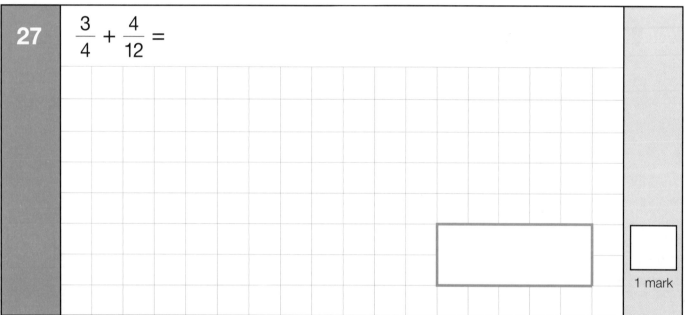

1 mark

28 $78.7 - 65.88 =$

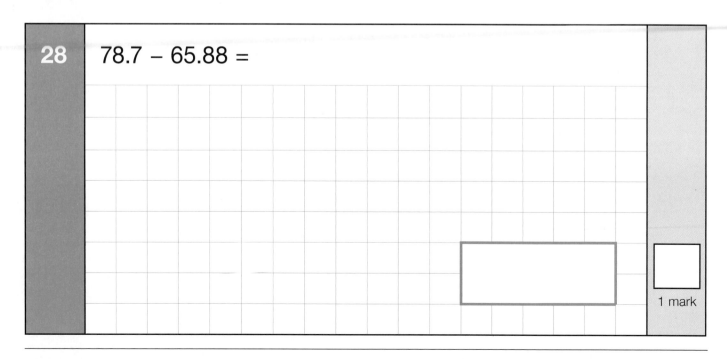

1 mark

29 $\boxed{}$ = 65 ÷ 100

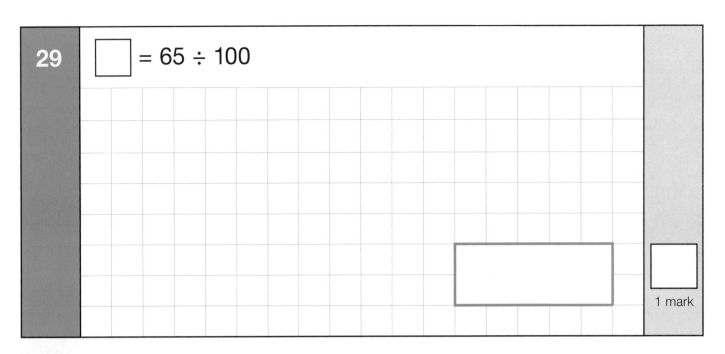

1 mark

30 50.806 − 32.661 =

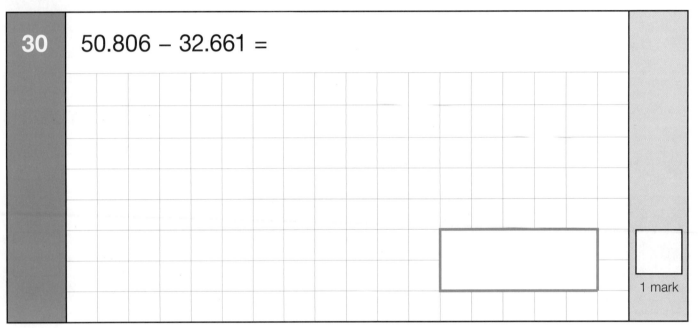

1 mark

31

Show your method

```
    5 7 3
  ×   4 5
  ───────
```

2 marks

32

$$\frac{3}{5} \div 4 =$$

1 mark

33

3 5 | 8 7 5

Show your method

2 marks

34

$40 \times 1\frac{1}{2} =$

1 mark

35

$$\frac{1}{3} \times \frac{1}{5} =$$

1 mark

36

56.77 − 5.777 =

1 mark

Key Stage 2

Maths

Paper 2: reasoning

You **may not** use a calculator to answer any questions in this test paper.

Time:

You have **40 minutes** to complete this test paper.

Maximum mark	Actual mark
35	

First name	
Last name	

Date of birth	Day		Month		Year	

1 This is part of a number square.

Circle the numbers that give a remainder of 3 when divided by 8

43	44	45	46	47
53	54	55	56	57
63	64	65	66	67
73	74	75	76	77
83	84	85	86	87

2 marks

2 Draw a pentagon with a pair of parallel lines.

Use a ruler.

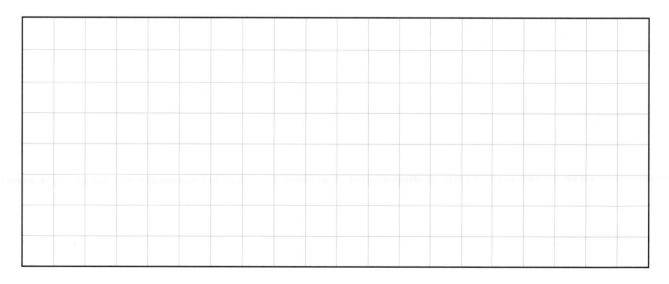

2 marks

3 Ellie and Rosie buy two pizzas.

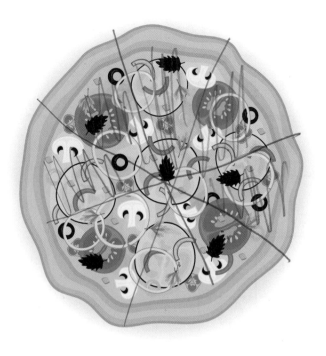 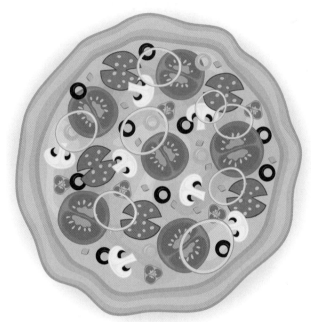

Ellie eats $\frac{5}{8}$ of her pizza.

Rosie eats $\frac{7}{8}$ of her pizza.

What fraction of one pizza is left?

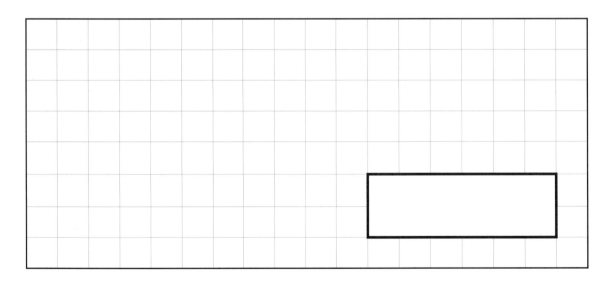

1 mark

4 Tick (✔) the two numbers that have a difference of 1000

32,658 ☐

33,758 ☐

33,768 ☐

34,758 ☐

43,858 ☐

5 Write the missing numbers in this calculation.

$$
\begin{array}{ccccc}
 & 5 & \square & 4 & \square \\
+ & \square & 5 & \square & 4 \\
\hline
1 & 2 & 6 & 0 & 0 \\
\end{array}
$$

6 Calculate the perimeter of this shape.

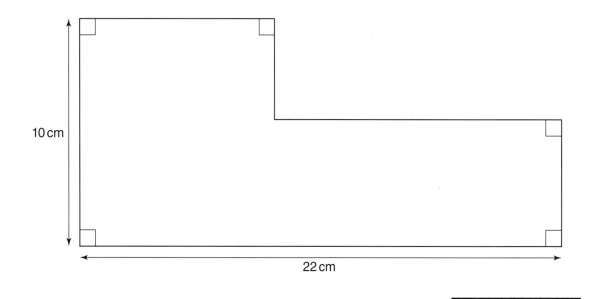

10 cm

22 cm

1 mark

7 A number squared and a number cubed both equal 64

Find the numbers.

$\boxed{}^2 = 64 = \boxed{}^3$

1 mark

8 Four hundred and sixty thousand, three hundred and five.

Write this number in digits.

1 mark

9

Reflect the shape in the mirror line.

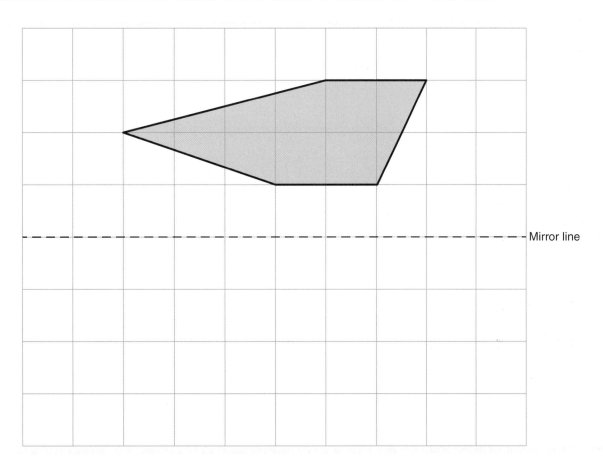

Mirror line

1 mark

10 This table gives approximate conversions between kilograms and pounds.

kilograms	pounds
1	2.2
2	4.4
4	8.8
8	17.6
16	35.2

Use the table to convert 7 kilograms into pounds.

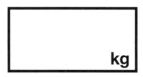

pounds

1 mark

Use the table to convert 22 pounds into kilograms.

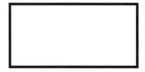

kg

1 mark

11 The attendance at a football match was 48,139

Two newspaper reports rounded this attendance in two different ways.

The Globe gave the attendance to the nearest hundred.

What was the attendance given?

1 mark

The Planet gave the attendance to the nearest ten thousand.

What was the attendance given?

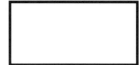

1 mark

12 Tick (✔) the largest number.

56.276   56.093   56.239   56.198   56.273

☐   ☐   ☐   ☐   ☐

13 Tom and Jack collect football cards.

Tom has 5 coloured cards to every 3 black and white cards.

If Tom has 36 black and white cards, how many coloured cards does he have?

Jack has 6 coloured cards to every 5 black and white cards.

If Jack has 36 coloured cards, how many cards does he have altogether?

14 330 ÷ 8 =

Give your answer as a decimal.

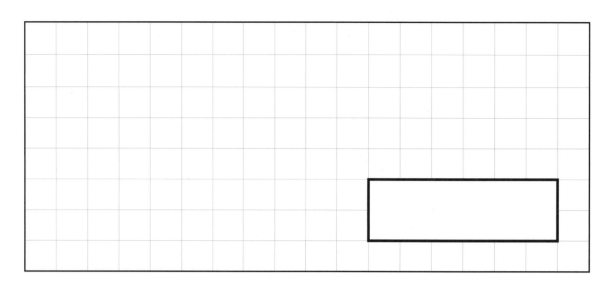

1 mark

15 Oakview School has 460 pupils.

40% are girls.

Sea Lane School has 240 pupils.

60% are girls.

How many more girls are there at Oakview School?

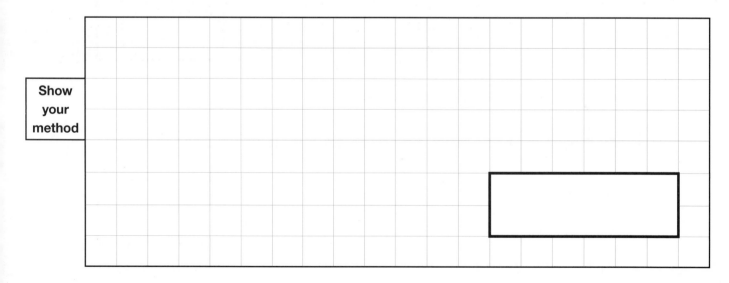

Show your method

3 marks

16 Find the value of $5a - 2b$, when $a = 5$ and $b = 7$

Find the value of $5a + 2b$, when $a = 7$ and $b = 5$

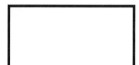

17 Here are two equations with missing numbers.

$$\square + \triangle = 18$$

$$\square - \triangle = 6$$

Work out the value of the missing numbers.

$$\square = \boxed{}$$

$$\triangle = \boxed{}$$

18 Here are four containers holding some water.

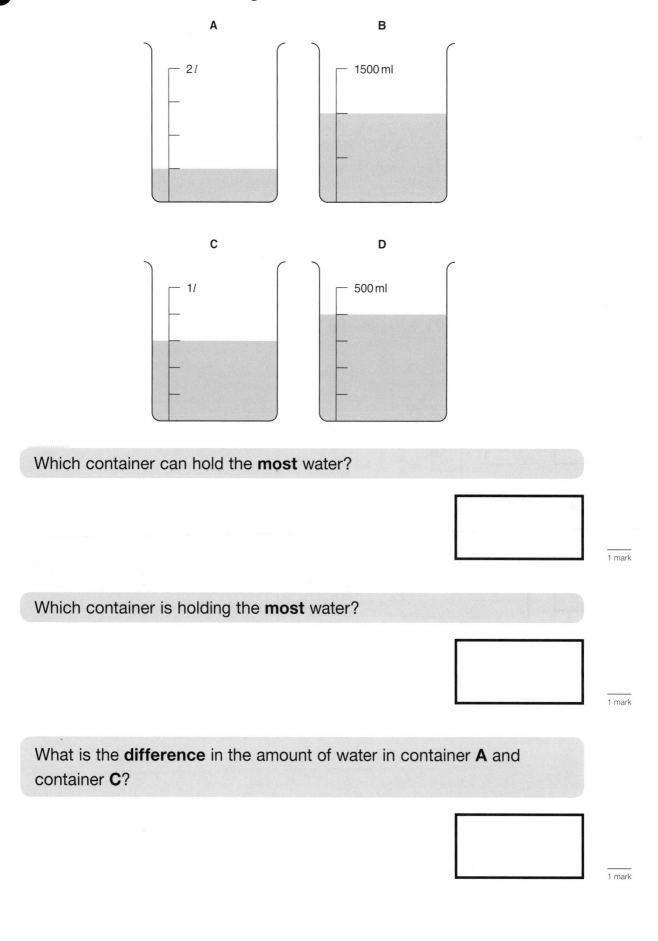

Which container can hold the **most** water?

1 mark

Which container is holding the **most** water?

1 mark

What is the **difference** in the amount of water in container **A** and container **C**?

1 mark

19 Tick (✔) the circle with a radius as a dotted line.

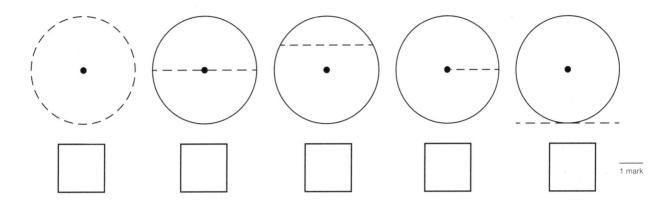

☐   ☐   ☐   ☐   ☐

1 mark

20 Here is a set of numbers.

7   15   24   30   48   53

Which two numbers are **common multiples** of 3 and 4?

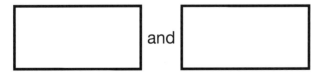

☐ and ☐

1 mark

Which two numbers are **common factors** of 60?

☐ and ☐

1 mark

Which two numbers are **prime numbers**?

☐ and ☐

1 mark

21 Sally wanted to go on holiday to Spain.

She compared the mean temperatures for UK and Spain.

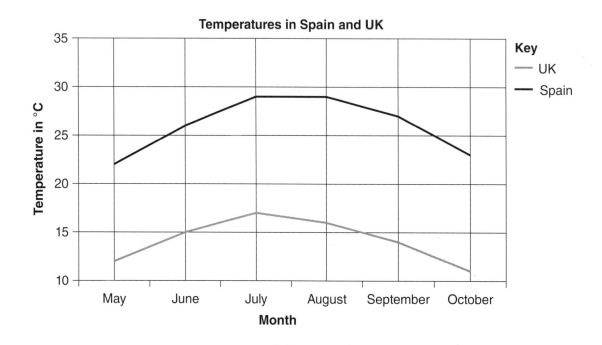

How much **warmer** was it in Spain than in UK in September?

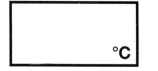

°C

1 mark

Sally wants to go to Spain when it is closest to 25°C.

Which months could Sally choose?

_____

1 mark

Key Stage 2

Maths

Paper 3: reasoning

You **may not** use a calculator to answer any questions in this test paper.

Time:

You have **40 minutes** to complete this test paper.

Maximum mark	Actual mark
35	....

First name	
Last name	

Date of birth	Day		Month		Year	

1   What number is shown by this abacus?

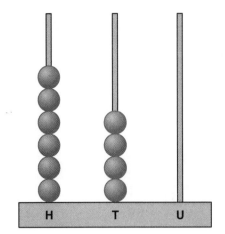

1 mark

2   Find the missing number.

$9 \times \boxed{} = 72 \div 2$

1 mark

3

What time is shown on this clock?

1 mark

4 Part of this shape is missing.

The dotted line is a line of symmetry.

Complete the shape.

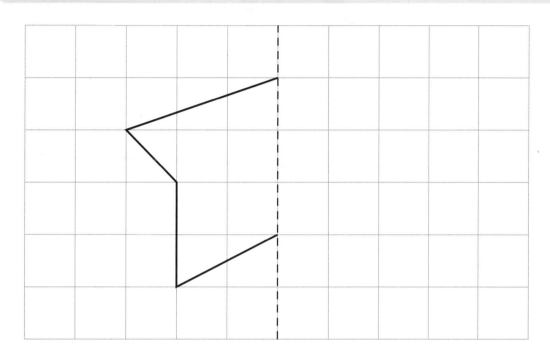

Draw the line of symmetry on this shape.

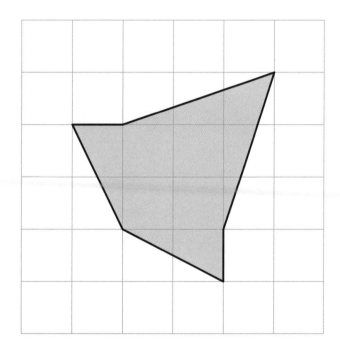

5 Chloe has 217 minutes left on her phone.

She uses 83 minutes.

She gets another 350 minutes.

How many minutes does Chloe have on her phone?

Show your method

minutes

2 marks

6 Tom buys 5 identical books for £26.

What is the cost of each book?

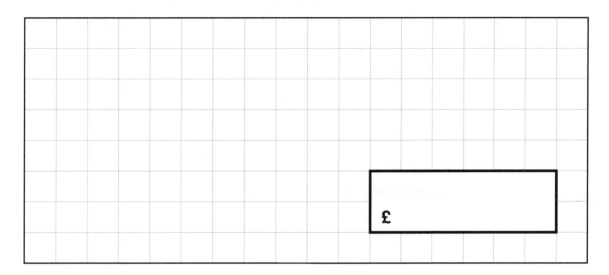

£

1 mark

7 1 inch is about 2.5 centimetres.

How many centimetres is 12 inches?

cm

1 mark

There are 12 inches in 1 foot.

There are 3 feet in 1 yard.

Is a yard shorter or longer than 1 metre?

Explain how you know.

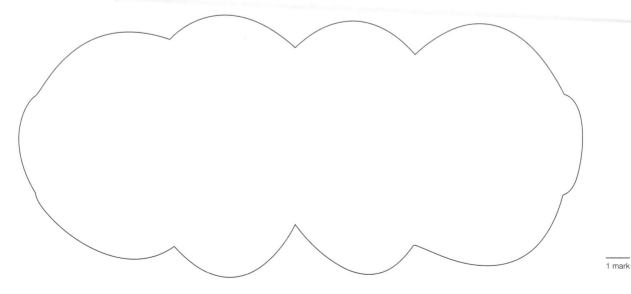

1 mark

8 The temperature outside a greenhouse is –4°C.

The temperature inside the greenhouse is 4°C.

What is the difference between the two temperatures?

°C

1 mark

9 Two prime numbers total 31.

What are the two numbers?

1 mark

List the prime numbers that are greater than 40 and less than 50.

1 mark

10 Manisha has 24 counters.

- $\frac{1}{4}$ of the counters are red.

- $\frac{1}{3}$ of the counters are blue.

- $\frac{3}{8}$ of the counters are green.

The rest of the counters are yellow.

How many yellow counters are there?

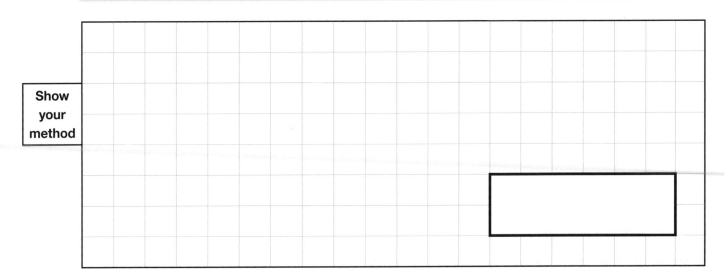

Show your method

2 marks

11 878,421 − 319,875 =

Round each number in this calculation to the nearest hundred thousand to work out an estimated answer.

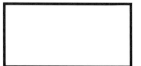

12 For each number, give the value of the digit 8.

7,376,548

8,065,913

5,682,790

7,368,514

13 An aeroplane is flying at a height of 8,000 m.

The outside temperature is −45°C.

Inside the aeroplane the temperature is 18°C.

What is the **difference** between the two temperatures?

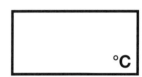

°C

1 mark

14 The population of a city is 275,386.

- 54,895 are aged 65 and over.

- 143,706 are aged 18 to 64.

How many are aged under 18?

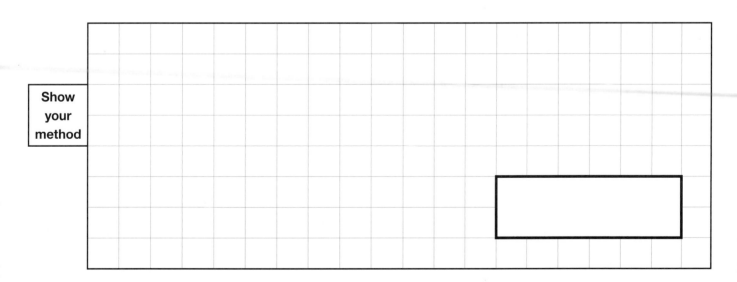

Show
your
method

2 marks

15 Draw a line from a fraction to the common factor used to simplify it.

$\dfrac{24}{30}$ 3

$\dfrac{21}{30}$ 4

$\dfrac{28}{32}$ 5

$\dfrac{20}{25}$ 6

2 marks

16 These two triangles are the same shape but different sizes.

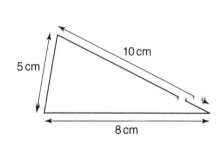
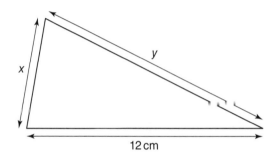

Work out the lengths of the sides *x* and *y*.

x = [ ] cm

1 mark

y = [ ] cm

1 mark

17 Write these lengths in order, **heaviest** first.

2.5 kg   200 g   2.05 kg   2,550 g   2.005 kg

1 mark

18 Tick (✔) each box if the fact about the drawn shape is true.

	has at least 1 pair of parallel sides	has at least 1 pair of perpendicular sides
Right-angled triangle	☐	☐
Rectangle	☐	☐
Parallelogram	☐	☐

3 marks

19 Teachers asked 120 children where they would like to go on a school visit.

This pie chart shows where they chose to go.

School visit

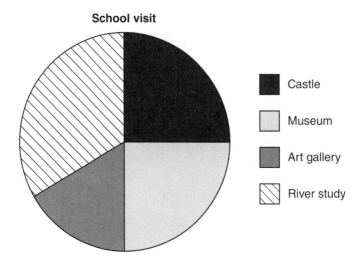

Castle

Museum

Art gallery

River study

> Estimate how many children chose to visit the castle.

1 mark

40 children chose the river study.

> What size angle at the centre of the pie chart is needed to show the river study?

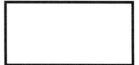

1 mark

Half the children chose either the river study or the art gallery.

> How many children chose to visit the art gallery?

1 mark

20 Abi sat 6 tests.

Her mean score was 45.

How many marks did Abi score **altogether**?

1 mark

21 A formula to find the perimeter, P, of a rectangle is

> **P = 2l + 2w, where l = length and w = width**

Work out the length of a rectangle that has a perimeter of 80 cm and a width of 10 cm.

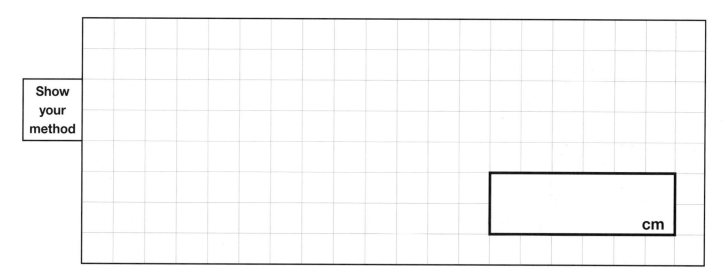

Show your method

cm

2 marks

Key Stage 2

Maths

Paper 1: arithmetic

You **may not** use a calculator to answer any questions in this test paper.

Time:

You have **30 minutes** to complete this test paper.

Maximum mark	Actual mark
40	

First name	
Last name	

Date of birth	Day		Month		Year	

1   40 ÷ 5 =

1 mark

2   828 − 102 =

1 mark

3 $\frac{7}{8} - \frac{4}{8} =$

1 mark

4 $\frac{1}{2}$ of 30 =

1 mark

5   888 + 1,000 =

1 mark

6   8,224 + 1,880 =

1 mark

7   765 ÷ 5 =

1 mark

8   0.6 × 100 =

1 mark

9   27,005 + 77,808 =

1 mark

10 $3^3 =$

1 mark

11 $4{,}088 \times 6 =$

1 mark

12 $12.45 - 8.49 =$

1 mark

13 0.03 × 6 =

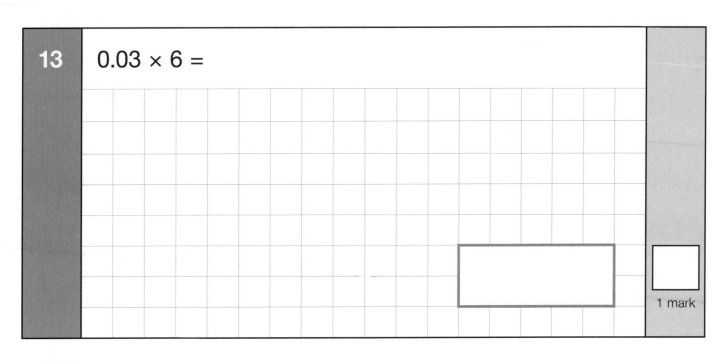

14 $\dfrac{1}{2} - \dfrac{1}{10} =$

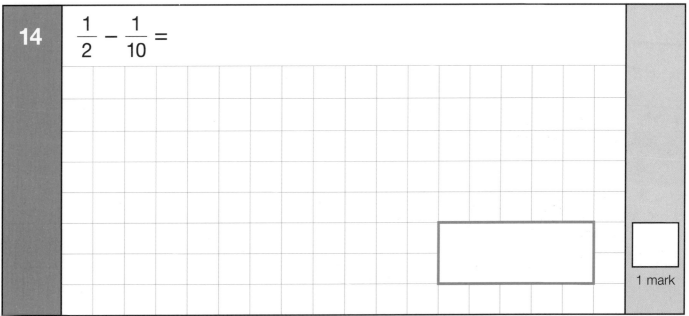

15 4 − 12 =

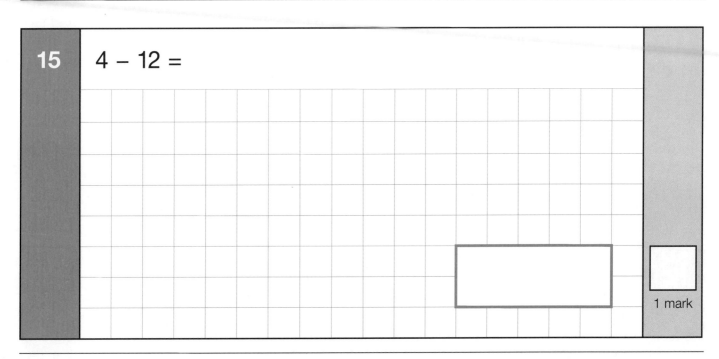

16   325.8 + 4.67 =

1 mark

17   80,000 – 8,000 =

1 mark

18 $\dfrac{1}{10} \div 2 =$

1 mark

19   690,360 − 251,069 =

1 mark

20   23.9 + 4.76 + 0.74 =

1 mark

21 $5\dfrac{3}{4} - \dfrac{3}{8} =$

1 mark

22 20 × 30 × 40 =

1 mark

23 30% of 3,000 =

1 mark

24 75 ÷ 1,000 =

1 mark

25

654.23 − 40.8 =

1 mark

26

Show your method

```
    1 8 2
 ×    6 2
 ─────────
```

2 marks

27

$$100 \times 2\frac{1}{2} =$$

1 mark

28

Show your method

$$2\ 2\ \overline{)\ 7\ 0\ 4}$$

2 marks

29 $40 + 10 \times 2 =$

1 mark

30

Show your method

$$7\ 1\ \overline{\rvert\ 1\ 4\ 9\ 1}$$

2 marks

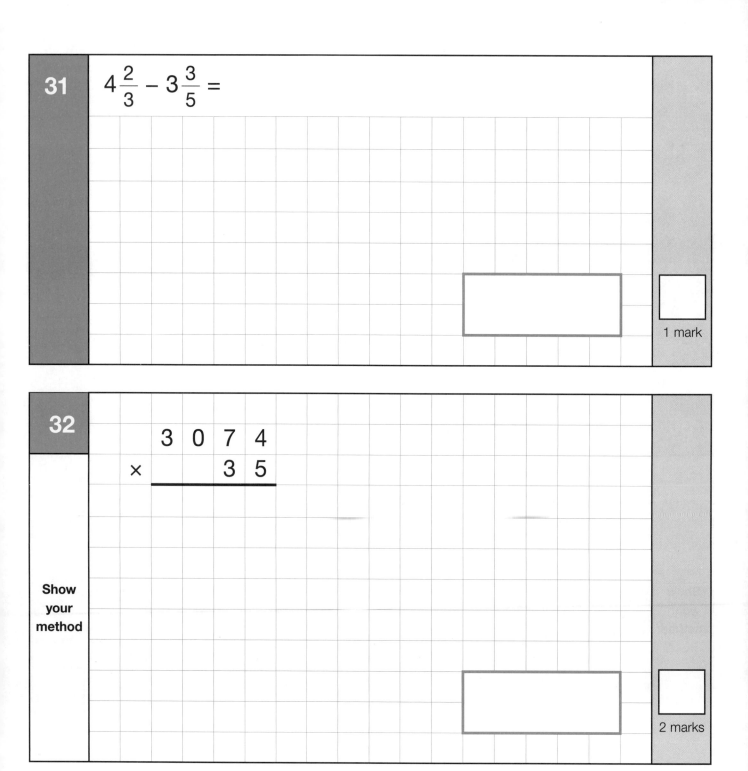

31

$$4\frac{2}{3} - 3\frac{3}{5} =$$

1 mark

32

Show your method

```
    3  0  7  4
 ×        3  5
```

2 marks

58

33 4,000,000 – 400,000 =

1 mark

34 78.357 – 6.05 =

1 mark

35 $\dfrac{1}{8} \times \dfrac{1}{5} =$

1 mark

36

$$\frac{2}{3} \div 2 =$$

Key Stage 2

Maths

Paper 2: reasoning

You **may not** use a calculator to answer any questions in this test paper.

Time:

You have **40 minutes** to complete this test paper.

Maximum mark	Actual mark
35	

First name	
Last name	

Date of birth	Day		Month		Year	

1   Tick (✔) the right angles in this shape.

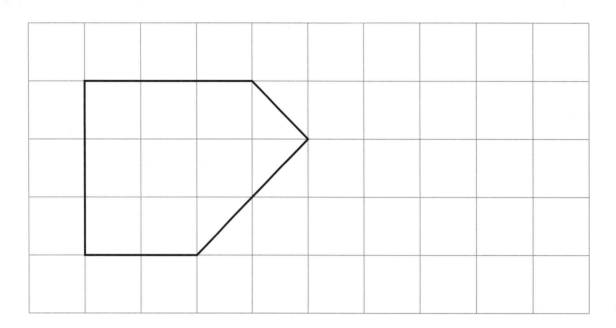

1 mark

2   Here are some counters.

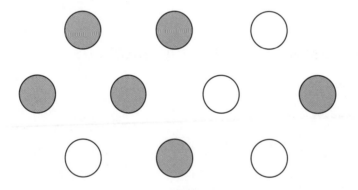

What fraction of the counters are grey?

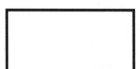

1 mark

3. Dev read 26 books in a school year.

He drew a graph to show how many books he read each term.

Complete the bar for Term 3.

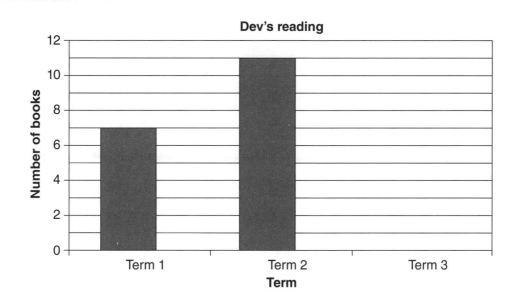

4 A train has 8 coaches.

Each coach has 72 seats.

The ticket collector says, 'I know 70 × 8 = 560'

What must he add to 560 to find how many seats there are in the train **altogether**?

5 Find the missing number.

64 × 24 = (64 × 20) + (64 × ☐) = 1,536

6 A square is drawn on an empty grid.

The coordinates of three vertices are marked.

What are the coordinates of the fourth vertex?

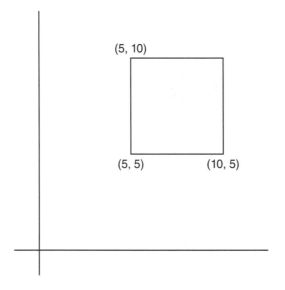

$$\left(\underline{\quad}, \underline{\quad}\right)$$

1 mark

7 A shop has a special offer.

Special offer!

Buy 3 tins of soup and get 1 free

Obi pays for 12 tins of soup.

How many tins does Obi get?

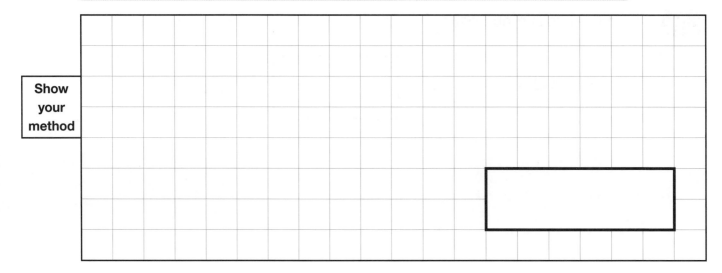

Show your method

2 marks

8 Max makes some concrete for a path.

For a path 8 metres long Max needs:

- 200 kg of cement

- 600 kg of sand

- 600 kg of stone

What weight of stone will he need for a path 20 metres long?

Show your working

kg

2 marks

9 Calculate the missing number.

$$56 \times 9 = 1{,}512 \div \boxed{}$$

1 mark

Calculate the missing number.

$$3 \times 8 = 72 \div 2 - \boxed{}$$

1 mark

Calculate the missing number.

$$56 + 64 = 3 \times 4 \times \boxed{}$$

1 mark

10 This table shows some approximate equivalent measures.

Metric	Imperial
2.5 cm	1 inch
30 cm	1 foot
90 cm	1 yard

Ula says, 'I am 5 feet 4 inches tall.'

How tall is she using **metric** measures?

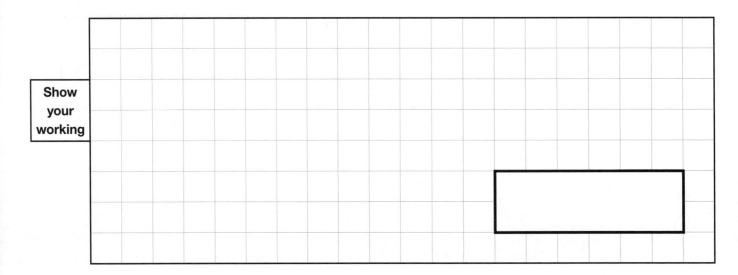

Show your working

2 marks

11 Here are some number cards.

| 4 | 4 | 5 | 5 | 6 | 6 |

Use the number cards to complete this equation.

Use each card only once.

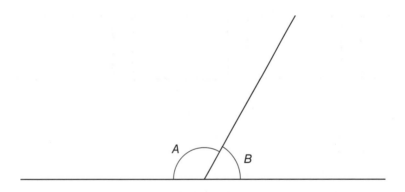 ÷ 100 = □ . □□

1 mark

12

What is the **total** of angle *A* and angle *B*?

□ °

1 mark

13 Here are two fair triangular spinners.

Each spinner is spun once and the numbers added to give a total.

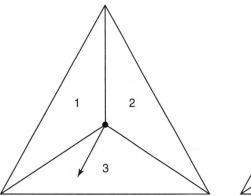 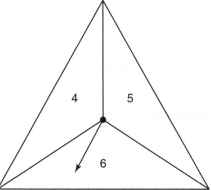

  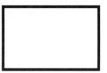 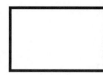

List the totals that can be made.

2 marks

14 This sequence decreases in equal steps.

Find the missing numbers.

6	−3			−30

2 marks

15 This is a net.

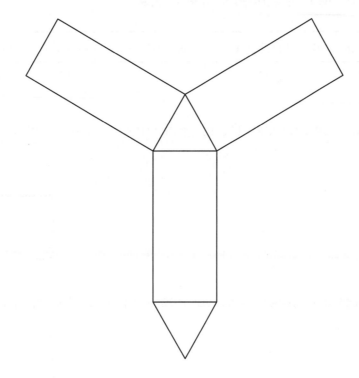

Name the 3-D shape.

_____

16 Josef is thinking of a six-digit number.

Josef's number has:

- Three hundred thousand
- Seven hundred
- Forty thousand

All the other digits are 6

Use these facts to complete the number.

17 This table shows the temperatures in five cities.

City	London	Belfast	Manchester	Cardiff	Glasgow
Temperature	4°C	0°C	–3°C	–1°C	–5°C

What is the **difference** between the temperatures in Manchester and Cardiff?

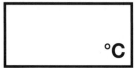

°C

1 mark

What is the **difference** between the warmest and coldest temperatures?

°C

1 mark

18 Find the missing numerators in these equations.

$$\frac{3}{4} = \frac{\boxed{}}{24}$$

$$\frac{5}{6} = \frac{\boxed{}}{24}$$

$$\frac{3}{8} = \frac{\boxed{}}{24}$$

$$\frac{2}{3} = \frac{\boxed{}}{24}$$

2 marks

What could the missing numbers be?

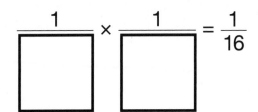

1 mark

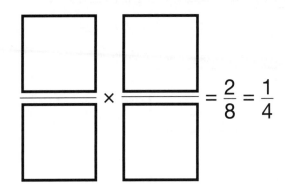

$$= \frac{2}{8} = \frac{1}{4}$$

1 mark

20 Dev and Sam share £45

Dev takes half the amount Sam takes.

How much do they each take?

Dev takes £ [ ]

Sam takes £ [ ]

1 mark

21 This rectangle has an area of 24 cm².

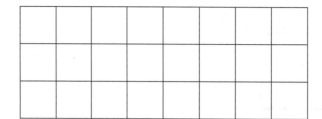

Write the lengths and widths of two different rectangles that also have the an area of 24 cm².

length [ ] cm and width [ ] cm

length [ ] cm and width [ ] cm

22 Angles *x* and *y* are equal.

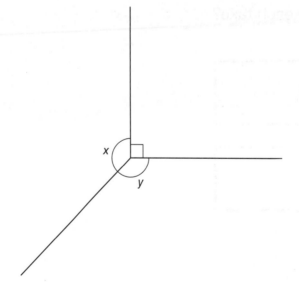

Calculate angle *x*.

X = [ ] °

23 Ben describes two shapes.

Name each shape.

My first shape has four
right angles and sides
of 10 cm and 5 cm.

_____

1 mark

My second shape has four
angles, two that are 120° and
two that are 60°, and sides
that are 10 cm and 5 cm.

_____

1 mark

Key Stage 2

Maths

Paper 3: reasoning

You **may not** use a calculator to answer any questions in this test paper.

Time:

You have **40 minutes** to complete this test paper.

Maximum mark	Actual mark
35	....

First name	
Last name	

Date of birth	Day		Month		Year	

1 Here are some number cards:

| 3 | 4 | 5 | 6 | 7 |

Use each card once.

$$\boxed{}\,\boxed{}\,\boxed{}$$

$$\boxed{+}\,\boxed{}\,\boxed{}$$

$$\boxed{6}\,\boxed{0}\,\boxed{1}$$

2 marks

2 This is a rectangle.

Tick (✔) **two** correct statements.

The two bold lines are perpendicular.	☐
The bold and thin lines are perpendicular.	☐
The two bold lines are parallel.	☐
The bold and thin lines are parallel.	☐

2 marks

3 Dom sells computer games.

This pictogram shows the number of computer games he sold one week.

Computer Game Sales

⊙ stands for four computer games

Sunday	⊙ ⊙ ⊙ ⊙
Monday	⊙ ◖
Tuesday	⊙ ◖
Wednesday	⊙
Thursday	⊙ ⊙ ⊙
Friday	⊙ ⊙ ⊙ ◜
Saturday	⊙ ⊙ ⊙ ⊙

How many computer games did Dom sell on Friday and Saturday?

games

1 mark

How many more games did Dom sell on Sunday than on Monday?

games

1 mark

4 Tick (✔) all the shapes that have $\frac{2}{3}$ shaded.

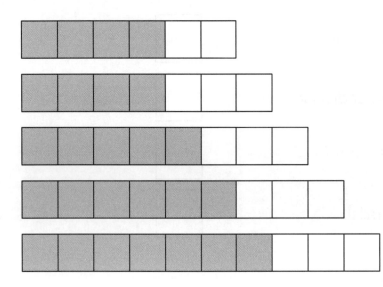

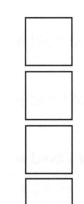

2 marks

5 Ned has a 10 kg bag of potatoes.

He uses 2.3 kg of the potatoes one day.

He uses 1,600 g of the potatoes on the next day.

What is the weight of potatoes left?

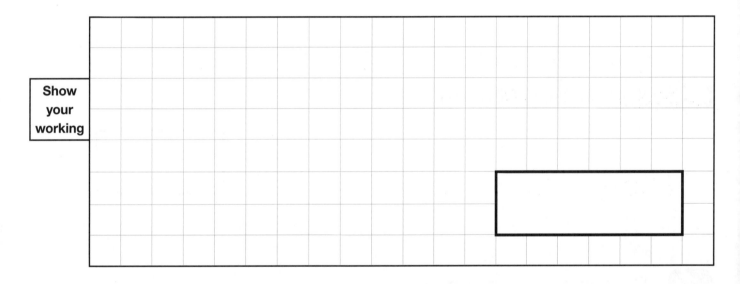

Show
your
working

2 marks

6   Translate the shape 7 squares right and 3 squares down.

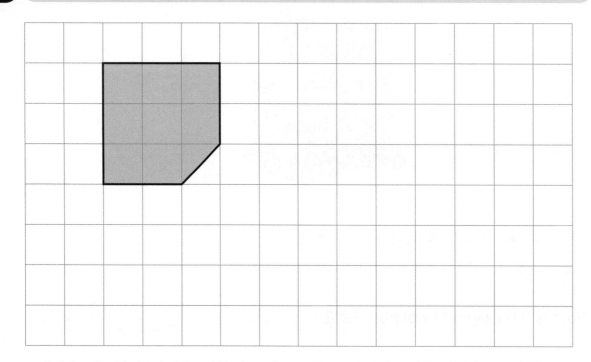

2 marks

7   Write the year MMXXII in digits.

1 mark

8   Circle the number that is both:

- a factor of 36

- a multiple of 12

9   18   24   36   72

1 mark

9 Round **196,704**

to the nearest ten

to the nearest thousand

to the nearest hundred thousand

2 marks

10 Complete this table of equivalent fractions, decimals and percentages.

Fraction		Decimal		Percentage
$\frac{65}{100}$	=		=	
	=	0.8	=	
	=		=	7%

2 marks

11 Write the following as digits.

one million, thirty-seven thousand, six hundred and four

1 mark

12 Here are three number cards.

| 1 | 2 | 3 |

Use each card to complete the missing numbers in these sentences.

Use each card only once.

5   is a prime number.

4 ⬜   is a common multiple of 3 and 7

3 ⬜   is a common factor of 62 and 93

2 marks

13 Find the missing number.

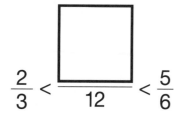

$$\frac{2}{3} < \frac{\boxed{}}{12} < \frac{5}{6}$$

1 mark

14 Tara thinks of a number, *n*

She adds 12 to the number and then multiplies the answer by 3

Tick (✔) the expression that shows this.

3*n* + 12 ☐

3(*n* + 12) ☐

3 × 12 × *n* ☐

36 + *n* ☐

n(3 + 12) ☐

1 mark

15 Measure the marked angle using a protractor.

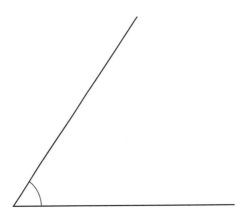

1 mark

16 Sam sat two maths tests.

These were his scores:

Paper 1: $\dfrac{14}{20}$

Paper 2: $\dfrac{18}{25}$

Change Sam's fraction scores to percentage scores.

Paper 1: [　　　　] %

Paper 2: [　　　　] %

2 marks

17 This pie chart shows the sports chosen by 80 children.

Here are some facts about the pie chart:

- 30 children chose tennis.

- $\frac{1}{4}$ of the children chose football.

- The same number of children chose gymnastics as chose rugby.

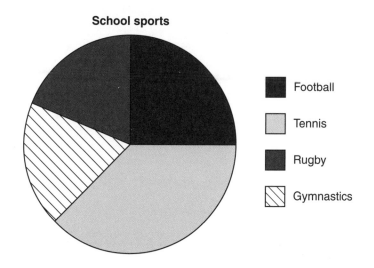

School sports

■ Football
□ Tennis
■ Rugby
▨ Gymnastics

How many children chose rugby?

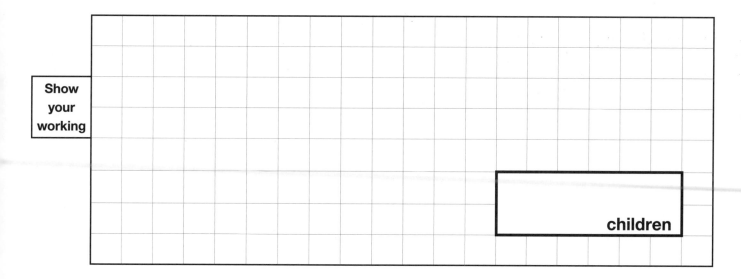

Show your working

children

2 marks

18 Tick (✔) the number with 7 as the hundredths digit.

6.497 ☐

64.97 ☐

649.7 ☐

6,497 ☐

64,970 ☐

649,700 ☐

1 mark

19 Work out the area of this triangle.

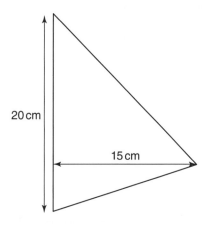

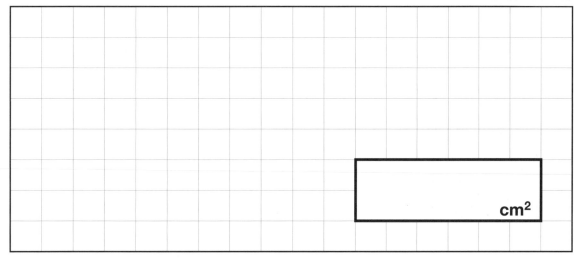

cm²

1 mark

Work out the length of this parallelogram.

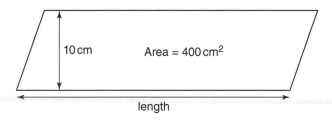

10 cm   Area = 400 cm²

length

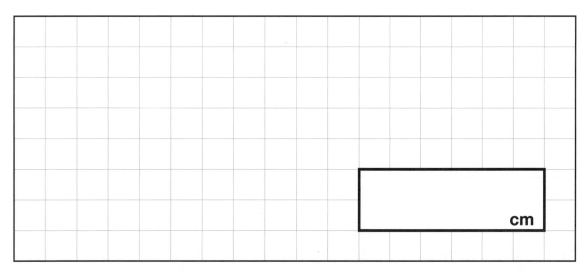

cm

1 mark

20 The dots, A to F, can be joined to make a straight line.

The dots are drawn at regular intervals.

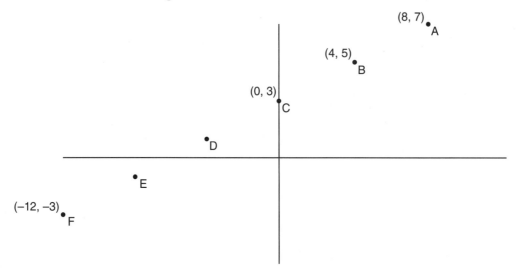

Some dots have coordinates.

What are the coordinates of dots D and E?

D = $\left(\underline{\quad}, \underline{\quad}\right)$

E = $\left(\underline{\quad}, \underline{\quad}\right)$

2 marks

21 Tickets to an amusement park cost £17.50 each.

There is a special offer. Eight tickets can be bought for £110.

How much cheaper is **each** ticket with the special offer?

Show your method

£

2 marks

Answers

Set A Paper 1

1. 215   (1 mark)
2. 630   (1 mark)
3. 1,334   (1 mark)
4. $\frac{4}{5}$ (Accept equivalent fractions.
    Accept 0.8)   (1 mark)
5. 8,999   (1 mark)
6. 3,434   (1 mark)
7. 1,821   (1 mark)
8. 0.81   (1 mark)
9. 77,930   (1 mark)
10. 25   (1 mark)
11. 3,115   (1 mark)
12. $\frac{7}{10}$ (Accept equivalent fractions)
                                    (1 mark)
13. –5 (Do not accept 5–)   (1 mark)
14. $\frac{9}{10}$ (Accept equivalent fractions)
                                    (1 mark)
15. $\frac{1}{6}$ (Accept equivalent fractions)
                                    (1 mark)
16. $\frac{1}{8}$ (Accept equivalent fractions)
                                    (1 mark)
17. 2.4   (1 mark)
18. 1,250   (1 mark)
19. 0   (1 mark)
20. 109,475   (1 mark)
21. 590,729   (1 mark)
22. 262.76   (1 mark)
23. 446.91   (1 mark)

24.

		2	3	4
	×		2	6
1	4	0	4	
4	6	8	0	
6	0	8	4	

(2 marks for correct answer. Award 1 mark for using long multiplication with no more than one error but wrong answer given. Do not award any marks if the 0 for multiplying by a ten is missing.)

25.

				2	4
2	3	5	5	2	
		4	6		
			9	2	
			9	2	
				0	

(2 marks for correct answer. Award 1 mark for using long division with no more than one error but wrong answer given.)

26. 3,075   (1 mark)
27. $1\frac{1}{12}$ (Accept equivalent fractions)
                                    (1 mark)
28. 12.82   (1 mark)
29. 0.65   (1 mark)
30. 18.145   (1 mark)

31.

		5	7	3
	×		4	5
	2	8	6	5
2	2	9	2	0
2	5	7	8	5

(2 marks for correct answer. Award 1 mark for using long multiplication with no more than one error but wrong answer given. Do not award any marks if the 0 for multiplying by a ten is missing.)

32. $\frac{3}{20}$ (Accept equivalent fractions. Accept 0.15)   **(1 mark)**

33.

```
          2 5
  3 5 | 8 7 5
        7 0
        1 7 5
        1 7 5
            0
```

(2 marks for correct answer. Award 1 mark for using long division with no more than one error but wrong answer given.)

34. 60   **(1 mark)**

35. $\frac{1}{15}$ **(1 mark)**

36. 50.993   **(1 mark)**

Set A Paper 2

1. 43, 67, 75, and 83 circled only.
   (2 marks: 1 mark for three answers circled)

2. **(2 marks: 1 mark for a shape with five sides; 1 mark for a pair of parallel lines)**

3. $\frac{1}{2}$ (Accept $\frac{4}{8}$ or other equivalent fractions)   **(1 mark)**

4. 33,758 and 34,758 ticked only.
   (1 mark: 1 mark for both correct answers)

5.

```
  5 [0] 4 [6]
+ [7] 5 [5] 4
-----------
1 2 6 0 0
```
   (1 mark: all correct for 1 mark)

6. 64 cm   **(1 mark)**

7. 8, 4   **(1 mark)**

8. 460,305   **(1 mark)**

9.

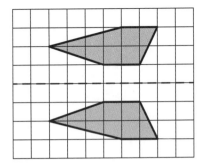

(Accept lines drawn to within 2 mm of vertices)   **(1 mark)**

10. 15.4 pounds   **(1 mark)**
    10 kg   **(1 mark)**

11. 48,100   **(1 mark)**
    50,000   **(1 mark)**

12. 56.276 ticked only   **(1 mark)**

13. 60   **(1 mark)**
    66   **(1 mark)**

14. 41.25   **(1 mark)**

15. 40

    (3 marks for correct answer. Award 1 mark for finding 40% of 460 = 184 or 1 mark for finding 60% of 240 = 144 or 1 mark for a correct subtraction of the answers even if the percentages are incorrect.)

16. 11   **(1 mark)**
    45   **(1 mark)**

17. ☐ = 12, △ = 6
    (2 marks for correct answer. Award 1 mark for ☐ = 6, △ = 12)

18. A   **(1 mark)**
    B   **(1 mark)**
    100 ml or 0.1 l   **(1 mark)**

19. 4th shape ticked only.   **(1 mark)**

20. 24 and 48   **(1 mark)**
    15 and 30   **(1 mark)**
    7 and 53   **(1 mark)**

21. 13°C (Accept +/– 1°C)   **(1 mark)**
    June and September   **(1 mark)**

Set A Paper 3

1. 640   **(1 mark)**

2. 4   **(1 mark)**

3. 7.20 (Accept 7.20 am, 7.20 pm, 19.20, 20 past 7)   **(1 mark)**

4.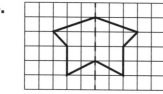

   (Accept lines drawn to within 2 mm of vertices. Ignore lines that are not straight.)   **(1 mark)**

   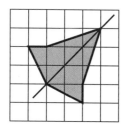

   (Accept lines drawn within 2 mm of the vertices.)   **(1 mark)**

5. 217 − 83 = 134;

   134 + 350 = 484 minutes

   (2 marks for correct answer. Award 1 mark for correct working, but wrong answer given.)

6. £5.20 (Do not accept 5.2)   **(1 mark)**

7. 30 cm   **(1 mark)**

   Explanation should show that there are approximately 90 cm (3 × 30 cm) in 1 yard and 90 cm < 100 cm   **(1 mark)**

8. 8°C   **(1 mark)**

9. 2 and 29 (Accept answers in either order)   **(1 mark)**

   41   43   47   **(1 mark)**

10. $(\frac{1}{4} \times 24) + (\frac{1}{3} \times 24) + (\frac{3}{8} \times 24) = 23$;

    6 + 8 + 9 = 23; 24 − 23 = 1

    (2 marks for correct answer. Award 1 mark for correct working, but wrong answer given.)

11. 600,000 (Do not accept 558,546)   **(1 mark)**

12. 8 or eight units or eight ones

    8,000,000 or eight million

    80,000 or eighty thousand or eight ten thousands

    8,000 or eight thousand

    (2 marks: 2 marks for four correct answers, 1 mark for two or three correct answers)

13. 63°C   **(1 mark)**

14. 275,386 − (54,895 + 143,706) = 76,785

    (2 marks for correct answer. Award 1 mark for correct working, but wrong answer given)

15.
    $\frac{24}{30}$ — 3

    $\frac{21}{30}$ — 4

    $\frac{28}{32}$ — 5

    $\frac{20}{25}$ — 6

    (2 marks: 2 marks for four lines correctly drawn, 1 mark for two or three lines correctly drawn)

16. $x = 7.5$ cm   **(1 mark)**

    $y = 15$ cm   **(1 mark)**

17. 2,550 g   2.5 kg   2.05 kg

    2.005 kg   200 g (Accept units that have been converted correctly, e.g. 2,550 g   2,500 g   2,050 g

    2005 g   200 g)   **(1 mark)**

18. right-angled triangle   ☐ ☑

    rectangle   ☑ ☑

    parallelogram   ☑ ☐

    (3 marks: 1 mark for each shape)

19. 30 (Accept +/− 1)   **(1 mark)**

    120°   **(1 mark)**

    20   **(1 mark)**

20. 270   **(1 mark)**

21. $80 = 2l + 2 \times 10$; $80 = 2l + 20$;
$60 = 2l$; $60 \div 2 = l = 30\,\text{cm}$

(2 marks for correct answer. Award 1 mark for correct working, but wrong answer given.)

Set B Paper 1

1.	8	**(1 mark)**
2.	726	**(1 mark)**
3.	$\frac{3}{8}$ (Accept equivalent fractions. Accept 0.375)	**(1 mark)**
4.	15	**(1 mark)**
5.	1,888	**(1 mark)**
6.	10,104	**(1 mark)**
7.	153	**(1 mark)**
8.	60	**(1 mark)**
9.	104,813	**(1 mark)**
10.	27	**(1 mark)**
11.	24,528	**(1 mark)**
12.	3.96	**(1 mark)**
13.	0.18	**(1 mark)**
14.	$\frac{2}{5}$ (Accept $\frac{4}{10}$ and other equivalent fractions. Accept 0.4)	**(1 mark)**
15.	−8 (Do not accept 8−)	**(1 mark)**
16.	330.47	**(1 mark)**
17.	72,000	**(1 mark)**
18.	$\frac{1}{20}$ (Accept equivalent fractions)	**(1 mark)**
19.	439,291	**(1 mark)**
20.	29.4	**(1 mark)**
21.	$5\frac{3}{8}$ (Accept equivalent fractions. Accept $\frac{43}{8}$)	**(1 mark)**
22.	24,000	**(1 mark)**
23.	900	**(1 mark)**
24.	0.075	**(1 mark)**
25.	613.43	**(1 mark)**

26.
```
        1 8 2
    ×     6 2
        3 6 4
  1 0 9 2 0
  1 1 2 8 4
```

(2 marks for correct answer. Award 1 mark for using long multiplication with no more than one error but wrong answer given. Do not award any marks if the 0 for multiplying by a ten is missing.)

27. 250 **(1 mark)**

28.
```
            3 2
  2 2 ) 7 0 4
        6 6
          4 4
          4 4
            0
```

(2 marks for correct answer. Award 1 mark for using long division with no more than one error but wrong answer given.)

29. 60 **(1 mark)**

30.
```
              2 1
  7 1 ) 1 4 9 1
        1 4 2
            7 1
            7 1
              0
```

(2 marks for correct answer. Award 1 mark for using long division with no more than one error but wrong answer given.)

31. $1\frac{1}{15}$ (Accept equivalent fractions) **(1 mark)**

32.
```
          3 0 7 4
    ×         3 5
    1 5 3 7 0
    9 2 2 2 0
  1 0 7 5 9 0
```

(2 marks for correct answer. Award 1 mark for using long multiplication with no more than one error but wrong answer given. Do not award any marks if the 0 for multiplying by a ten is missing.)

33. 3,600,000 **(1 mark)**

34. 72.307 **(1 mark)**

35. $\frac{1}{40}$ (Accept equivalent fractions)

(1 mark)

36. $\frac{1}{3}$ (Accept equivalent fractions)

(1 mark)

Set B Paper 2

1.

(1 mark: all three right angles needed for 1 mark)

2. $\frac{3}{5}$ (Accept equivalent fractions, e.g. $\frac{6}{10}$, decimal, 0.6, and percentage, 60%) **(1 mark)**

3. A bar or line drawn to show 8

(1 mark)

4. 16 or 2 × 8 **(1 mark)**

5. 4 **(1 mark)**

6. (10, 10) **(1 mark)**

7. 12 ÷ 3 = 4; 12 + 4 = 16 tins

(2 marks for correct answer. Award 1 mark for correct working, but wrong answer given)

8. 20 ÷ 8 = 2.5; 600 × 2.5 = 1500 kg

(2 marks for correct answer. Award 1 mark for correct working, but wrong answer given)

9. 3 **(1 mark)**

12 **(1 mark)**

10 **(1 mark)**

10. 30 × 5 = 150; 2.5 × 4 = 10;

150 + 10 = 160 cm

(2 marks for correct answer. Award 1 mark for correct working, but wrong answer given)

11. Accept any correct answer, e.g.

456 ÷ 100 = 4.56; 465 ÷ 100 = 4.65;

546 ÷ 100 = 5.46; 564 ÷ 100 = 5.64;

645 ÷ 100 = 6.45; 654 ÷ 100 = 6.54

(1 mark)

12. 180° **(1 mark)**

13. 5   6   7   8   9

(2 marks: 2 marks for five correct answers, 1 mark for three or four correct answers)

14. −12   −21

(2 marks: 1 mark for each correct answer)

15. triangular prism **(1 mark)**

16. 346,766 **(1 mark)**

17. 2°C **(1 mark)**

9°C **(1 mark)**

18. $\frac{3}{4}$ = $\frac{18}{24}$

$\frac{3}{8}$ = $\frac{9}{24}$

$\frac{5}{6}$ = $\frac{20}{24}$

$\frac{2}{3}$ = $\frac{16}{24}$

(2 marks: 2 marks for four correct answers, 1 mark for two or three correct answers)

19. Accept $\frac{1}{2} \times \frac{1}{8}$ or $\frac{1}{8} \times \frac{1}{2}$

or $\frac{1}{4} \times \frac{1}{4}$ or $\frac{1}{1} \times \frac{1}{16}$ **(1 mark)**

$\frac{1}{2} \times \frac{2}{4}$ or $\frac{1}{1} \times \frac{2}{8}$ (Accept for either calculation numerators or denominators reversed) **(1 mark)**

20. Dev takes £15

Sam takes £30 **(1 mark)**

21. Possible answers are:

length   24 cm   width   1 cm

length   12 cm   width   2 cm

length   6 cm   width   4 cm

(Accept lengths and widths reversed. Accept fractions and decimals if correct, e.g. 48 cm × 0.5 cm. Do not accept length 3 cm width 8 cm)

(2 marks: 1 mark for each pair of correct answers)

22. 135° **(1 mark)**

23. rectangle (Accept oblong) **(1 mark)**
parallelogram **(1 mark)**

Set B Paper 3

1. Possible answers – 567 + 34,
564 + 37, 537 + 64, 534 + 67
**(2 marks: 1 mark for correct placing of
7 and 4 in the units column)**

2. 2nd and 3rd boxes ticked only.
**(2 marks: 1 mark for each correct
box ticked)**

3. 29 games **(1 mark)**
10 games **(1 mark)**

4. 1st and 4th shapes ticked only.
**(2 marks: 1 mark for each correct
box ticked)**

5. 10 – (2.3 + 1.6) = 6.1 kg or 10,000 –
(2,300 + 1,600) = 6,100 g (Accept 6.1 kg
or 6100 g. Units must be correct, e.g.
do not accept 6.1 g or 6,100 kg. Accept
6,100 or 6.1 without units.)
**(2 marks for correct answer. Award
1 mark for correct working, but wrong
answer given.)**

6.

**(2 marks: 2 marks for drawing as
shown; 1 mark for correctly orientated
and sized shape translated 7 units
right or 3 units down)**

7. 2,022 **(1 mark)**

8. 36 circled only **(1 mark)**

9. 196,700
197,000
200,000
**(2 marks: 2 marks for three correct
1 mark for two correct)**

10.

Fraction		Decimal		Percentage
$\frac{65}{100}$	=	0.65	=	65%
$\frac{4}{5}$ or equivalent	=	0.8	=	80%
$\frac{7}{100}$	=	0.07	=	7%

**(2 marks: 2 marks for six correct
answers, 1 mark for four or five
correct answers)**

11. 1,037,604 (Accept misplaced
commas) **(1 mark)**

12. 53
42
31
**(2 marks: 2 marks for three correct
answers, 1 mark for two correct
answers)**

13. 9 **(1 mark)**

14. 2nd box ticked only **(1 mark)**

15. 55° (Accept angles within 2°) **(1 mark)**

16. Paper 1   70%
Paper 2   72% **(2 marks)**

17. $\dfrac{80 - (\frac{1}{4} \times 80 + 30)}{2}$ = 15 children
**(2 marks for correct answer. Award
1 mark for correct working, but wrong
answer given)**

18. 2nd box ticked only **(1 mark)**

19. 150 cm² **(1 mark)**
40 cm **(1 mark)**

20. D   (–4, 1)
E   (–8, –1)
(2 marks: 1 mark for each coordinate)

21. £17.50 – (£110 ÷ 8) = £17.50 – £13.75
= £3.75
**(2 marks for correct answer. Award
1 mark for correct working, but wrong
answer given)**